The Cursed Book

Do not read this

Dyna H Solar

#12YearsChallenge

Chapter 1 Those who took the bait

So, did you buy it? Really? Well, that's interesting. Now let's discuss why you would. Most likely you just wanted to have a little peek inside because you were curious about the dark malevolent side right? Congratulations it's always people like you in horror movies who the audience shouts at to not open the freakin door. But do you listen? No. And ta-da the only time you get chosen first is by a ghost. *Ouch*

Or maybe you bought it because you don't believe in all this spooky stuff and wanted to prove it to yourself and everyone else. Again congratulations, you are that one character who refuses to believe in ghosts, and downplays all the strange occurrences and warnings, until it's too late. And you end up being the 'pre-first' victim. The example of what not to do. Just like life makes you one. *Double Ouch.*

Fair warning: I have a sarcastic personality, so more roasts are to come. I recommend keeping some aloe on hand to apply to your roasted behinds. Yes, no crude words will be used here. I am keeping this book very demure, very mindful but not cutesy so expect to read an impeccably immaculate inimitable issue. And no, I totally did not use a thesaurus to write that. Shut up.

You could also be a wise young professional since much more experienced ones won't even have the time to look at this. They are busy with work, family, and finding time to rest and not read. Not to say they don't read but only the refined, suggested and recommended ones. Not the exploratory kinds, unless they are avid readers themselves.

Or you could also be a carefree student. I mean, your assignments are still pending, your grades are experiencing a roller coaster ride that keeps going down, and your degree is on the line. If that doesn't matter to you, why would a book title? Yes, the personal attack here is real.

Now the next type of person to read this book could be, well, someone who does worship Satan maybe? Or just like all the mystical occult things? So overall not really frightened with the title of this book.

But in any case sorry to say you have been fooled. All my understanding of spookology - yes it's a word - is based on watching famous horror TV shows and movies. So yeah nothing. But let me just sprinkle some holy water here just in case...

But if you are not any of the above, which means you acknowledge such material, get terrified by something even remotely paranormal, and still bought this book, then just one question: Geez, who hurt you? Why would you do that to yourself?

I am talking to you who watches creepy Instagram reels hiding behind the chat. You, who watches horror movies knowing very well it will haunt you for days, knowing you will be sleeping with the lights open at night and still get petrified over the tiniest noise in the house.

Chant god's name when you get too scared? Or for Indians, chant Hanuman Chalisa? Stick with a person closely so that you both can somehow fight off a ghost? When in reality ghosts rarely attack unless you are all alone. But it doesn't help much when you experience sleep paralysis and can feel that sinister stare on yourself, does it?

Another must-do is to keep your legs from hanging out of the bed. Have that big blanket cover you completely like it's some holy shield a ghost won't be able to cross? With earnest intent. Why? Have you not seen enough horror movies where the blanket is snatched away first?

Don't forget some ghosts have diplomas in advanced technology for affright and they will directly come into the blanket. Yeah, then you are face to face with a ghost with nowhere to go or escape their ghosty breath. Since ghosts are dead beings and devils are associated with everything unpleasant and many times associated with the smell of rotten corpses I think it's safe to assume that their breath would stink! You will not just get your soul annihilated but your final moments will be filled with an utterly disgusting smell you will be forced to inhale.

And for all the sisters with brothers, it would be like the air dissipated from your brother's behind that they purposely release in your room while laughing evilly, just 10x worse with no escape. I mean who knows maybe you'd faint off the horrible smell first before the evil spirit even kills you.

Anyway for those who believe in dark energy (Negative energy kind not the cosmological one) or curses (spirits kind, not jjk anime ones. If they existed I would be on a quest to find Gojo or become one) I love being arrogant but in a good way.

Your stance here is not the issue but your thought process might be. You have one life and you still felt like, 'You know what? I might feel there is a ghost right behind me for days, I might get haunted but this shit is more important. (Just look behind you, I know you want to)

Also not that I am complaining. I am not in the least bittersweet. Buy more. Gift this book to your friends and family too while you are at it. They will enjoy it too!

Chapter 2 Why I wrote this book

Now that you have read this book, and realized the book is absolutely nothing about what the title says you may realize to not judge a book by its cover. Lesson learned right? But if I had a plain boring title you were most likely to not read this. You took the bait because the title intrigued you.

So the real reason to write this book? It's an experiment. This book is just another strategy, a new writing style focusing on commerciality. Why? I have already published a book before. A fictional, medium-paced, filled with emotions novel but it did not turn out to be a great success.

And I am a very ambitious person. Ambitious enough to keep trying and stubborn enough to prove myself. I am a full-time learner, a full-time founder, a full-time startup manager, a full-time artist, a full-time author, and a full-time finance professional (Not 6 '5, not blue eyes, and definitely no trust fund. If I did you wouldn’t have even heard from me)

So this is my new idea to try since I am currently working towards the life I want to have. My options as any young professional are limited. My choices are: 1) Further studies in a top school, which is expensive, requires extensive preparation, and also gives you more debt than job opportunities. 2) Work on a job you don't really like and doesn't seem worth the money you get either.

Or my favorite 3) Pray to God. Specifically for a miracle to go back in time, a couple of years back when you saw the ad to buy bitcoin, but you scoffed and opened your book to study for your 30-mark chemistry unit test, consisting of topics I don't even remember anymore or need. And yes I got a perfect score, yes I still remember, yes I still have the marked answer sheet but I still wonder what if I just had amused myself then and bought it. How fun would that be...*sigh*

Anyway, what if you don't want to play by those rules anymore? You know, what if you kick away all the traditional paths and make your own way instead. How do we do that? I say be creative and make your own way to success. You don't have to follow the crowd. You certainly don't have to do what worked for others. Maybe now it's better to build your own path to get the life you want instead of walking on the footprints left by many.

I have not yet given up on my previous writing style but am simply trying this new one which is much more straightforward to write. Why? Because I am not moronic enough to keep pushing against a wall. Though it's a different story if you are drunk, the wall would move.

People don't read just good books anymore, they read good & different books. They prefer something new, something unique, something to grab their attention quickly, and something out of the box. Remember the key here to win is smart work not hard work.

Not gonna lie if this book sells great and goes on to be a bestseller. I would be a little annoyed. But extremely ecstatic too. Why annoyed you may wonder? Because I wrote this book in exactly 1 month! The other books I have written took 3-4 months to complete and then an additional 1-2 months to edit, design, and finally publish. But this one, all that was done in under 1 month. See smart work, not hard work!

There were irregular working hours during this month. It was not as if I wrote every day, but sometimes I worked more than the other day too. One day instead of writing two pages I just increased the font size by 1 resulting addition of 6 pages. So now I have completed my writing target of 3 days. Laziness? Maybe but since I am optimistic I view it as being smart as a whip. Happy Thoughts :)

Ps: Just today I increased the paragraph spacing to get 12 additional pages. Scintillating huh? Not to brag but corporate can't handle me.

This is what I would advise anyone out there. You have got a good job already? Good. You saved money to invest? Better. You have utilized your hobby, time, or interest to generate a second income? You won!

My passion for writing started when I was in high school. I actually never liked any classic books when I was younger. I first started reading those dumb fiction stories online like any teenager and then switched to better books to finally realizing why classics are 'classy' and should be treasured.

What led me to write though was reading those better books in between where I hated how some books ended abruptly or led to a 'happy ending' which was not so happy in my understanding. Yeah, it frustrated me to the point I had to write my own books to read. Become *Elite*.

Writing is my second passion, not my first priority. I am just using all those high school interests and hobbies that we think don't really matter anymore or provide us with a real job to get favorable results. But now that we can see so many social media influencers getting paid in millions, letting go of their university tags,

‘Real’ jobs, and judgment from family, relatives, & society are thriving which has definitely changed the whole perspective from working to survive & save for retirement to having financial security all the while you actually enjoy what you do!

Now I am not saying you quit your jobs and start writing/painting/influencing nope. Don’t quit your jobs, not yet at least not till you have a solid second income. In fact, some of you might even want to continue doing your job if you really like it. The purpose of having a second/backup career is just in case some unfavorable situation happens to the first job.

Imagine that you worked hard on multiple projects and now at the end of the year, you got to know your other colleague who barely worked or maybe did a good job but not comparable to yours, hmm... you can feel that motivation slowly melting away leaving you numb. Questioning why do I even bother anymore? What is the purpose? Let's say you endured it once, but what if it happened again? Now is when you quit.

Any uncomfortable/unfavorable issue that you cannot clear without having to apologize for a mistake you did not make or putting on a smile for any senior who is rude and disrespectful. Wouldn't it feel good to quit such a place without having to worry about the money later? It's like asset allocation, but only with your time. Don't spend 100% of your time & energy on just one job. If you do, you better be getting paid like crazy with no high risk of burnout & termination!

Well said, "Don't put all your eggs in one basket" Have different pretty colored baskets so that even you feel bonita when you admire them!

Now let's say you have a hobby you want to commercialize, the eminent factor to focus on here is to put your heart into it. The genuine efforts. It doesn't matter if you barely have 20 min for it, what matters is if it's just for those 20 minutes, were you completely focused on the task?

You have to always put your heart into your work no matter what you do, and of course, consistency which stems from discipline.

Discipline is that calm rational noiseless whisper that keeps our heads clean. No unnecessary questions, no what-ifs wondering, and no what people are thinking about me. Rather, even if all those negative voices start talking in your head, Discipline is the cold commander that says, “Keep your mouth shut” and protects us. And when you can’t focus it says “(Your name) LOOK AT ME!” Yes, I am romanticizing discipline here. Are you starting to feel kinda…? All that I do for you guys.

Also, I cannot emphasize enough on the importance of being *different*, And no you don’t have to try so hard to do it just let your personality scream! And no I don’t mean be different from other guys/girls. No one wants that. I mean be differently creatively. Because guess what each one of us is already different in our own ways. Sometimes the difference can be as minute as the style in which we share the stories many find relatable.

Don't let your shyness & hesitation stop you from speaking up and letting your personality shine!

Anything I write in this book is not so unique I know. It is not really meant to be either, just relatable enough is okay. What I did differently would be the presentation. The informal yet authentic tone. The image I created is different from its content, something that grabs attention immediately yet the content is intriguing enough to keep people engaged and of course the marketing. My marketing team is just me. Don't worry my ambition can handle it all. No wonder I only attract people with daddy issues. Oh sorry! Do you feel called out here? hehehe.

Another thing about the lessons from this book is that anyone can write it. Yes, you can. It's simple, literally any thought in my head is being put into words here without over-thinking much.

But what actually matters here is that many people can write but only some would. And out of those, only a few would complete it till publishing while most would leave it in between, and then only a handful would brand it in a quirky and creative manner to make it stand out further.

Now it's up to what to do next! (Note; This does not only apply to writing but any ideas of yours.) It could be the very same idea you wrote years back in your diary or at the end of your notebook thinking I will look into this in the future. Start working on it today. The sun has risen, you must not be still asleep!

Chapter 3 Horror Movies

Do you like horror movies? Also which kind? The supernatural ones where there is an actual ghost or the serial killer ones?

In simple words, are you someone who finds it intellectually stimulating to explore themes of death, the dark side, or black magic OR do you like watching the darker side of human nature? Like watching a man or woman finally snapping and killing? Because these two are very different kinds of horror movie enthusiasts.

Of course, there are some movies with a combination of both where the killer turns out to be possessed by an evil spirit or a demon but wait in the final scene you get to see a human (probably) wearing a black robe with pale skin and veiny hands doing some rituals that we realize it was that chihuahua (I am being mindful enough to not write the B-word) who was behind it all to achieve its mission of bringing evil on earth.

You know to open the door of hell and let the demons escape, which makes it safe to assume that many have been successful so far. Cause when I take a look at the news, it's almost enough to make one believe that hell really might be empty.

Sometimes you also wonder if evil souls/demons knew about all the inhumane crimes that we hear about almost every day and might be actually afraid of us? Because unlike them, we have a heart, a soul, a mind, and most importantly feeling & empathy.

Unfortunately, we are becoming humans filled with wicked emotions and have let go of everything positive to live on greed and pleasure alone. Demons might not even want to come out anymore. They just might be sitting and thinking what do they need us for exactly? Want to think about it for a while? Take a pause, and choose to be good humans.

Raise your hand if you are someone who randomly starts thinking of world problems, and their possible solutions only to realize you need to become someone capable enough first so that you are in a position to help those who are in need.

This makes me glad that humans like you do exist! Stay safe, healthy, and in good company! The world needs more people like you.

Now back to the movies and their cliche plots. Let's start discussing the red flags. No, we are not talking about your crush. And don't you dare pretend to be colorblind either. Hell, even a colorblind person can tell a red flag when they come across one. Don't even try, you chihuahua. (Why Chihuahua? Well since your little frame can hardly handle that big attitude of yours!)

In our list of obvious red flags first comes:

1. The abandoned asylum/ the remote cabin/ haunted house.

Now why would you even want to go there? There is no network, no power, just some souls chilling there.

I never understood why was it necessary to go in at all? I mean there is a reason why no one (Human) is living there right? Cuz have you seen the rent these days! A huge abandoned mansion with its dark academia and gothic aesthetics among crazy gen-z who would even give afterlife trauma to the dead for not giving their share of rent in this cursed economy??

But hey they are also kind enough to recommend a therapist to process the trauma. After all, mental health comes first. So the Gen-z will approach the ghost in a three-step way:

First, approach the ghost with food and make inappropriate jokes about death to break the ice.

Second, spill the tea which includes spilling of tea from both sides. Rant about your life, your day, and your friends, especially that one friend who got back together with their ex.

Third, decide to become friends and roast the hell out of the ghost which would make them die of shame again as their fashion is outdated, they have no skincare routine, and worst of all they have the choice to rot in bed but somehow don't and decide to haunt, that too in this cold weather?

Imagine the ghost spilling the tea of how it was betrayed by their closest friend or lover after a Gen-Z bullied him to share it because they're not giving aura.

Once the tea is served, a lesson is to be learned
Ghost them before they ghost you first

The same goes for the abandoned asylum in the middle of nowhere. Get a hint! Even the crazy people could not survive there! And the only reason *the little group* goes there is for some adventure. No, you human! It's a group application to the afterlife.

Living life on only two brain cells is already adventurous enough. Let's not try to prove Darwin's theory right any further now.

2. And the epic, don't open the locked door part.

You see satanic signs all over, you see a freakin cross upside down but nah what could possibly go wrong right? Have you ever paused and thought about what could possibly go right? What would you even gain from going inside? This is why a hobby is needed guys.

All that unsettled chaos in your head that feels unruffled when there is finally some chaos outside to feel so that you are too busy doing that you have no time to think. Well, go to a therapist. Start meditating. Don't open doors, you can't close. This is not just limited to horror movies, this is a golden life lesson. Learn and apply.

Don't do things you know can never have a good end. Don't indulge in bad habits that you may not be able to control. Don't do drugs or entertain alcohol when you don't want to but give in to peer pressure. Don't let bad company affect your sense of right and wrong.

3. Virus/curse that makes people act like crazy and they come out at night. The parents always close the doors but a child will always open it.

I never understood why a child would be so welcoming to someone so creepy-looking. A normal child would scream and run. Or these kids have never watched a horror movie before, they were just directly born in one. This is why it's important to make them watch, so the next time they know what is a normal smile and what is an unsettling one. So they run away from the ghost, not smile back and say '*Look Mommy it's my new friend*'. Sure they might get nightmares first but it's worth it if it keeps them safe at the end of the day right?

Another life lesson, learn the consequences of your actions, don't do things just because you feel like it. Think! Think twice! And then if you still make a mistake learn. Slowly you will know whose smile is fake and whose is genuine.

Another method to stop the child from opening the door? The Asian Mother. Oh, they don't even need to speak, one stare and you know you messed up. When I was a child I would never and especially not ignore my mom. This is where gentle parenting goes wrong and the next thing you know either there is a killer after you or someone has been possessed.

Asian mothers are built different. The truth is even if it's your relative you will look at your Asian mom first to see if she knows who is here and is okay with you opening the door for them. She is the boss. And she knows it.

Now with an evil spirit and an Asian mom in the same house who to be scared of exactly? Answer honestly if the floor has been mopped freshly, and there is a ghost chasing you will you really take the risk of walking on that floor? Wouldn't your first reaction be to jump across, the safer option? Or the alternative is to just give up. You don't win anyway.

Life lesson: The Asian mom here is your trusted partner, your friend, your mentor, your family, or even just your experience that stands proud next to you. It stops you from getting scammed, or betrayed. They help you avoid mistakes. Because no, you don't need to make mistakes every time to learn and grow. Be wiser, observe other people's mistakes, and learn not to make the same.

4. Another cliche is the little group of friends.

The leader who suggested it in the first place, the girl who is in love with one of the friends and throughout the movie is focused on him talking & laughing and not the ghost lurking behind her. To all of the people who have a blind one-sided crush, it's okay to love but not to be stupid in love. Unless you want your tombstone to read, 'The one who got ghosted figuratively and literally'

Sigh...Knowing Gen-Z they might actually find this funny and start planning the exact opposite of what I said. Guys seriously don't or your fathers will be hearing from me. And you know how difficult it is to find a missing person right?

There is also the idiot who decides to go out on his own to explore. The crazy one of the group sometimes ends up being the first victim or sometimes they end up finding something cursed like in a book, some toy, a picture, or worst of all a doll. The creepy doll they still just have to pick up to chuckle at and then throw it away. Funny right? Another funny moment was when you went away and its eyes followed you.

I am not just talking about horror movies for no reason here, all these lessons can be applied to stop your life from becoming a horror film. Always remember it's not just you but also those around you who shape the way you think, for example when in a jungle with no network, doesn't matter if it's a haunted house or if it's just some cannibal living there or even if it's literally nothing. Don't split up. Your hair has already done it. Don't be sorry later, be smart now.

What defines aura? Imagine a masked villain who is indestructible, who survives impossible injuries. Who, most importantly, calmly walks and still catches up to its victim. It's a life lesson here humans. Of course not literally, but be that person, keep your eyes on your destiny, don't overshare, be calm, be patient and you will reach your goal soon. Most importantly you will look freakin cool as you get there. In simple words, have an infinite aura. Don't just grab your iced oat milk latte with caramel drizzle imagining you are the main character, become one and don't care about the extras in your life (With all due respect).

Or you could choose to be the other person the frantic one, the one who has a lot of time on his hands but wastes it doing unnecessary worrying and makes a complete idiot of himself, trips and keeps on tripping because they don't learn from their mistakes they just want to get to the door they aren't prepared to open. Would you prefer being the first type or going through so much worry and anxiety? Or in simple words have an immense negative aura.

No aura would be a person who has let go of his ambitions, stopped dreaming or maybe still does but not a single thing to try. A great piece of advice to those who have friends/family or co-workers like this, don't ever listen to their advice. You shouldn't listen to someone who gave up on their dream to stop you from achieving yours.

Special mentions to the flashlight hero whose batteries die the second the screams start and would open for only a glimmer of a second for you to catch a glimpse of the ghost (i.e. don't give up too soon!). Another would be the individual who trips over literally nothing (i.e. give up, it's not meant for you). Horror movies would never be the same without them.

Chapter 4 Gen-Z

It's said those who like horror movies have a higher tolerance for fear and anxiety. Is that true for you or are you just a Gen-z?

I feel they have a lot of generational trauma they face, and the best freakin quality about them is that they are not willing to pass it on to the next generation. They know what has happened to their parents, what has happened to them and they are not willing to transfer that trauma to the next generation. No, sir, no such cycle will be repeated anymore. Gen-Z is eating trauma for breakfast, getting constipated, and living in their own delusion but will not pass it off to the younger ones. Also, their younger ones are cats & dogs. No, not the gender kind, the pets.

After seeing how society functions it makes complete sense why they don't want to get married, at least not because they HAVE to, only if they want to. Same for having kids, they know it's not need to HAVE them to get a fulfilled life but rather because they want to and can give a child complete love & care.

I genuinely admire this. All mistakes, and shortcomings of the previous generation seemed to be corrected by the next one.

Gen-Z refuses to work in jobs they hate, doesn't matter how socially admired that role is. They will leave a high-paying 12-hour job to work comfortably in pajamas with a latte and a dog on their lap to make pretty digital planners and sell them online. Or choose to become vloggers, or content creators to share what they love.

But the absolutely essential quality about them is they speak up! Whether it's at work to set boundaries by putting a professional smile on their faces to say "My working hours are 9 to 5, you call me then. Actually don't call me, instead just email" or fight climate change right after they figure out how to recycle that pile of Amazon boxes from their shopping spree.

Their tone never fails to impress. They question not just you but sometimes your whole existence (in a good way, because let's face it some people do need to apologize to the trees for the oxygen they waste). And the absolutely important topic, “Mental Health” They will not let others hinder their peace, they do enough of that themselves. They don’t just want to avoid meeting people but also want to avoid their thoughts.

They normalize saying ‘no’ instead of politely agreeing. They know when someone crosses a line and aren’t afraid to say, “Anything that comes out of your mouth is only useful for compost”.

So what if Gen-Z has a playlist for basically everything? Yes, they have a playlist for working out, for studying, for sleeping, for cooking, for cleaning, for bathing, for getting dressed, for walking, for driving, and even for crying. Yes, they will cry but make sure the songs in the background are giving the vibe. They will feel the main character energy getting hurt today but they will rise and make them all pay by becoming the richest coldest fashion designer/CEO/mafia gang leader or something along the line.

Or maybe they will just read a book about it, imagine it in their heads before sleeping, or listen to another playlist titled, "You Are the Most Powerful Villain"/ "When You've Had Enough".

It's okay to cry but it's also important that we look aesthetic as it happens. Cause what do you mean cry & be aesthetically unpleasing? What do you mean the people living in my imagination are not witnessing this scene and feeling my pain? What do you mean this won't be written in my biography as the turning point in my life? Hey! Their pain is real!

They respect others' opinions and listen to them. They listen and *they judge.* Then they tell their best friend/sibling about the same and judge together. But you know something isn't matching when they don't judge their actions as much as their sign. "Hey, I heard he burned down his house! Yeah well, I am not surprised he is a Scorpio."

#Justiceforscorpios I don’t know what they did but this is the general attitude towards them on social media. Hence why they need to know your sign for Scientific Purposes. Which sign do you think I am? I like being mysterious. So none of you will get it right.

They also take astrology really seriously and will use it to justify anything. Anything literally. Why did the Gemini cancel the meeting? Actually, they didn’t, it was their twin. The twin in their head. Ah, got one for you to guess the sign: “We don’t get involved in drama. We *create* it when we need to."

Now let’s get to coffee, we all know how many coffee lovers are present today. Some of you might be reading this book while drinking coffee or thinking about having one. But let's be honest here, how many of you actually like coffee, and not basically sugar drinks? No, I am not talking about your iced-vanilla latte, extra cold brew, almond milk, with a dash of cinnamon, no foam order. I listen and don’t judge. I write & declare war.

Anyhow, Gen-Z doesn't subscribe to negativity. No, they believe in manifesting, so are more likely to subscribe to a Gemstone channel. They believe in vibe culture and manifesting ritual aesthetics. Yes, their gemstones, their candles, mysterious music, and digital vision boards. They are the modern witches.

They trust the universe, despite having serious trust issues, which is completely understandable after the many "we're just friends" texts. Don't cry here please, take a tissue and wipe those tears. I am not trying to attract any negativity here. I manifest positive vibes only, and money, success, and abundance because I am worthy :)

But overall Gen-Z is smart, they are creative and they find beauty in everything. They are so generous to even overlook the red flags and still love the other person. Yes, the drinking, the talking to ex, the 'I am different from other guys/girls'. Yes, they will still accept you. And yes they will try to fix you. When that doesn't work you better mute this person on all social media because not only thousands of posts are coming your way about self-worth, self-love, and independence. But you will also be witnessing the cycle of sad songs to healing songs/revenge songs (Depending on the personality) to finally feel-good/empowerment anthems.

But you know what they absolutely love from every possible angle? The black flags. They won't even try to fix it on the contrary they actually worship them. They are not just beautiful to them but heavenly. They want to breathe them, they want to burn for them, they want to be absolutely devoted to them.

They don't care about anything they do. No, not even murder. What *murder*? (read this in a British accent) They just went on a dark path once but that doesn't define them. They are more than just the few crimes they did. Yes, they are also sociopaths.

I blame all the TV shows/movies in which they made the villains hot. You should have given them both a bad personality & looks. But you gave them a terrible personality and absolutely sizzling hot looks. This is what is called a lethal combination. And if they are smart? In a 'I can find a thousand ways to destroy you without even lifting a finger' way. Dammm that's the double lethal combination.

And then you find all these people on social media asking where to buy a 1000-year-old vampire with anger issues or that one toxic black flag villain with an IQ over 180. He may kill them, but they will let him, she may ruin them but they will let her with a smile for even being in her presence.

This devotion to self-destruction is present vastly in our adorable Genz. This chapter did not have any lessons, if you can find one on your own go ahead. That if you are smart enough to see what others don't. Not everything will be spoon-fed to you here. You can share on social media too, I will be watching you all.

But sometimes it's okay to take a break and have fun. This chapter was just for that. All little roast for you all, cause I know you like to use humor to cope with stress & anxiety.

Yup, some insulting jokes, laughter, and public humiliation along with coffee sounds like the perfect evening.

Chapter 5 A horror: Job interviews

These are a series of horror movies. But then there are horror interviews, moments where life flashes in front of your eyes as you wonder how in the world I forgot the name of the company I was interviewing for?

This is a common occurrence for those who are desperate for a job, they don't see titles anymore, if they meet the eligibility criteria they will apply or sometimes if the job title sounds close to it they will apply blindly. Now this comes down to all those who are searching for a job in today's market. Desired role? Desired company? Desired pay? Hah, never heard of it. Maybe a look at those rejection emails is needed to refresh the memory.

All those, "Thank you for applying…." emails. The fact that you don't even need to read after the thank you to know they have politely told you to go find something else to do. But jokes on them, they don't know after so many rejections you're numb to it. Rather you have gotten braver because you will apply again using a different email and phone number to fool the system. It could be a completely different person with the same name, same educational background, same resume and same IP address right?

You are not fooling anymore by being casual in your first application and then going all Shakespeare for the second with a different email.

Another thing that candidates dislike is the LinkedIn gurus who post, “How to get a job in 2 month” (the grammatical error is intended) or “Read this post if you want to get a job this 2 weeks” Jesus, someone give a call to the ministry of employment, they have it all wrong because apparently this is all it takes to be employed! What do you mean there aren’t enough jobs created for the young population? Have you not read their post?? How dare you not believe it and refute it with logic? No, we never heard of economics.

The other would be the Career Coaches, some are okay, they understand your goals and will try their best to get you there & even reach out to their personal connections as much as they can. Some are there to refer you in exchange for money, and some are there to get a job that you would have gotten anyway but they will make it feel like a big deal and promise you that they will help you get your dream eventually but you will have to pay them more but they will make sure you get it this time. Yes, you must trust them completely and give them all your savings.

Everyone is creative these days, they have found different sources of income. So now it is more on you to spend money carefully, sometimes having too many options is a bit of a headache. Just like how you have so many OTT subscriptions but nothing to watch and end up watching the same show for the 27th time. You may not get an office but you compromise & just watch it.

And then one day you get a phone call/email and it's the round one interview. Happy dance, till you see it's that same personality test and online assessments that you must have given a thousand times now. You hate your life, you sigh & realize they already took your previous results into consideration and oh that means you must be getting that rejection email soon too. You now make a different email account to apply for jobs.

This time you performed better on the assessments you passed, and now you get the face-to-face interview round.

Nervous, a little bit because you really want this job, you have prepared those lines singing the praise of the company, your motivation, & especially the answer to the question, "Why this role?".

If you get lucky and your interviewer is nice, great. Some will be very warm, and kind, and ease your anxiety and some may not exactly be that kind and smiley but are pookies from the inside and will try to give you hints or frame the question differently. You may think you blew it but that cold interviewer who seemed the least interested in the meeting actually gave you good feedback and now you are invited for the next round. Yay!

And as usual 4-5 rounds of interviews which were initially supposed to be 3. Now instead of 1 month, it took 2 months to get to know the final result. Sometimes I wonder if the company just can't decide who to select and just decide to play 'let's see who lasts the longest' and just select that person? It's quite possible.

Now comes the case if the interview is not so nice. This could be the very smiley and warm interviewer who had warmth in his eyes but judgment in their heart. You didn't even know but when you said your GPA they judged you, when you said your college name they judged you again, when you said subject, again judgment and when you talked about previous projects & the company you worked at, they smiled and said your work sounds amazing but had already moved on to open the resume of the next person in line for the job.

Another type could simply be the cold ones who are extremely strict with their requirements. If you don't answer what they want to hear, the interview ends and you know it. Still far better compared to the other as now even if you blame yourself, you know what to work on next.

Some not-so-nice interviewers could also be biased. Yes, the ones who will interview you but only for a formality. They have already made up their mind to select the ones from their alma mater, or their friend's friend, or their family's friend. How to know if you have this type of interviewer? Just go ahead and ask a question about the company or the role. This person would sigh and not give you a proper answer, something along the line, "Well depends, there is no simple answer...". They don't care to answer in more than a line and must be wondering why answer when they are not getting a job anyway?

And then comes the competitive interviewer. Oh, this one is really interesting. I've had this one before. They may pass you or they may not. It depends on their ego. This interviewer will not ask you questions to see if you know, but rather boost their own knowledge & how much they know.

They ask you difficult questions, but will say, "I am going to ask you very easy questions." No, you won't, but if somehow you do answer that, they will *add* their input for sure, something to show how smart they are. If you answer wrong, they will chuckle with a small eye roll that says, 'I knew it, no one is smarter than me anyways'.

They may or may not answer before they come up with another question, a difficult one again if you don't answer a rejection, but if you do answer both the questions correctly. Ah, now that ego is hurt because you know more than them when they were your age.

Once the technical questions are over they will try to attack you again with the personal round interview questions. 'Why did you study this? Don't you think this subject is less important than XYZ in terms of giving actual results?' (This is not a question just for business, and humanities people but also for STEM people. Yes, not all STEM degrees are treated equally. There is an order of ranking present there too.)

Or ‘if this subject is really this great why didn’t you go for a role more related to that? Oh, do they not make good money there?’ Or the classic ‘your previous work isn’t something that excites me much, why should I hire you?” And the list goes on.

Don’t worry darlings it’s not you, it's them. They are just afraid one day you might become more important than them. How about proving them right?

Chapter 6 Running out of topics

Okay so Let's take a break. I will think of something to write on.....Or should I just add some 'spot the differences' pictures here to keep you occupied? Just kidding. I seriously am running out of topics though.

This chapter will be about ***procrastination***! Now now don't run away from your friend. Say hi, no don't cuddle with it either. Let's not get too friendly here. Your books & pending projects are starting to get jealous. They see you & they judge you silently. If you get quiet you can hear it, the whispers...in your head if you still give a damm, if you have already reached the point where you don't? Well, umm, continue reading.

Procrastination. You know you have it when even saying or typing the long word makes you feel like not writing anymore. Hey, guys can't we have a shorter version of it? Prelay, delay, offput? Offput sounds like a rapper's name. You decide or let me know any new ones you have in mind.

(P- Procrastination from here on)

P is because of many reasons. But the one I can talk about is when things don't go your way. You keep trying but you don't get the results you want. You imagined your life would be different but nothing has changed much? Then we hear our inner voice that says 'What's the point when it's not going to work anyway' but then another voice that says 'No don't give up yet, maybe this is it?'

Your motivation hits rock bottom, you start to wish if only luck was on your side maybe things would work. As you see it has been working for others who don't even try that hard right?

What is the way to get out of this? I'm not sure either. Everyone operates differently. We can try some methods though like shifting to another activity, by taking a break, starting a new hobby, or just going on a vacation to clear up your mind.

We could also start another project for a while. Maybe one that can be done in a shorter duration? That can help give you some sense of gratification so that your motivation boasts up again.

But if you don’t ever want to depend on motivation in the first place then be highly disciplined. Disciplined enough that it's now a muscle memory to just get up and complete the tasks you have set for the day. The longer you live a life judged by discipline the longer you will be free from the fluctuating burdensome motivation.

It's never too late to build discipline though. You can start even today but let's be honest you won’t, discipline is like *Soma* drink (a sacred beverage) whose ingredients are unknown. No one can tell exactly what's needed to make it, but everyone has their own theories. Sometimes people spend too much time just wondering rather than doing anything. That’s another problem. But those who have figured it out for themselves are living well.

Many after reading this would just wonder of a life they want that could be achieved through discipline. And maybe a 100 maximum out of 100 million actually would do something about it, the rest of the people will just feel a motivational boost for a few hours, a few days, or a few weeks. Then you just forget it. But of course not true for all, there are a few gems who will promise to start tomorrow, and then they will think what's one more day gonna do? Let's start from the next day, then well let's start from next week maybe? And once the next week also comes. Next month it is! The 1st of the month which later turns out to be the 1st of the next year...

Now you know how the story goes on right? And no I am not even gonna talk about those who wait for the 1st of a new year falling on a Monday. Listen to me, this is not you. I can fix you. (No one can fix you, not even your delusions)

But just so you know I am not trying to criticize you either. Trust me the reason I am able to write this is because I have dealt with it as well.

If you still are trying to change, if you still feel irritated, or frustrated it's because you want to change. Heck, even while reading these lines you felt it in your heart. That’s all needed. Don’t be too hard on yourself, there is a lot you went through too and it will be okay as many would give up on themselves but not you, you still have the will to change.

Because you know you don't want yourself to be lost, because you don’t want to live a life full of regrets when you could have achieved your dreams, be that first billionaire in your family, and be free from ever having to worry about money and achieve all your goals!

The potential of yours is the reason why you feel extremely agitated when you waste your time that you could have utilized better and then you feel even more burdensome due to your guilt that the rest of the day gets ruined anyway right?

How to come out of this loop? A really fitting solution could be a ‘comradely’ where a close friend keeps check on you! Because let's be honest even though we are giant adults sometimes we need someone to guide us back on the right path. Sometimes don't you wish that your future self could come back to the past and just really rebuke you, set you right, and make you work? I know it's not just me!

This is where your 'comrade' comes into play. Someone who will help you set your goals, and have a bit of a 'tough love' approach to make sure you complete what you started. Wouldn't that be good? Now who could be this comrade? The best one would definitely not be your parents. No, we know how that goes. (Especially for Asian kids, I don't even want to imagine what would happen to you guys.)

The best one could be your sibling. Your really close friend? Best friends too can work if they are not too supportive. Since they might just accept your excuses for being too understanding. Yes, I am talking about those friends who would even jump in the well with you because it seemed like a fun story to tell later.

Another approach, it's a little darker but may work for some. It is "Scare yourself". Imagine in the future, if you choose not to work today. I know you only want to have good vibes but let's take a dive into this. Your worst nightmare. When you are stuck in a situation where you can't help but just regret things. Why didn't you do this earlier, why didn't you take this seriously then? When there is no option left but to struggle to survive and watch others get the dream you wished to achieve.

Now snap out of it. You have time, it's not too late yet. Get going with your dreams, don't just daydream anymore, start living it from today. But I feel sometimes you may need a little scare just to realize how much every fiber of your being wants to achieve that one dream. Don't forget that feeling.

Now that I have typed all the solutions I had in mind, let's discuss more about why we procrastinate in the next chapter. You should know you are not alone here, you're not some hopeless loser you keep telling yourself at times when it gets tough or you experience a major fallback. Or when you don't work up to your expectations or how on some days don't work at all. You can do it!

Eliminate your distraction by conquering your mind. Don't just lock away your phone to reduce your screen time. Conquer your mind first. Control your mind to the point where your phone could be right in front of you and yet you wouldn't pick it up. I know you are wondering how to do that, but you already know, we all know how habits are eventually fixed and all the different methods you have read about online can help. But you have to try it to know it.

Start meditating (it does make a difference, there are papers supporting this) and be with the right people who can inspire you too. Remember all who you want to make proud, remember the person you envision yourself to be, and remember your worst nightmare if you don't work on yourself today. And most importantly remember the fire of ambition that lights up inside you because of how much you want to achieve that one dream.

Yeah, that one persistent annoying nagging dream that will only stop bothering you once the day comes that you finally have it in your hands. When you know this, who the heck can make you give up?

Chapter 7 Fighting Our Battles

There are many reasons why one may procrastinate. But I can only talk about specifically those who were always diligent and then out of nowhere it started.

This one is a bit tricky, right? What really changed? You were always in the top 1% of your class in school, you did amazing even in extracurriculars back then why don't you even want to get out of bed now?

Could it be that what you were working for is something you don't really want but society says that's how you make it in life right? You know the usual, 'that's how it is, deal with it. Everyone who succeeded in life did it, you should too.'

Anyone who thinks this way: Respectfully scram! Never can the same path work for everyone. Now of all times, you need to create your own. Never judge those you don't understand because you have not been in their shoes, don't throw meaningless words at them thinking you know better. Heck, even if you have been through a similar situation and had a certain reaction to it doesn't mean everyone would react the same. Don't be that assuming imbecile.

We all are designed differently, think differently, and work differently. Some may look at an apple falling to the ground and eat it, some may not pick it because they just don't like apples, some may start planning to pick them all to sell them, some may not even notice it, some may start playing catch with it, some may just admire the beauty of nature and draw it, some may admire it & write a poem and some may get curious and end up formulating the theory of gravity by observing an apple falling from a tree.

This is the reason why no one can have any one strong method of making it in life. Who knows what might work for one and might be just a complete waste of time for the other? We need to try different things, we need to appreciate our own style too.

Don't know how many might find it useful. But here is a simple system that is adaptable for many uses.

The 3-6-9 system

(1-3)
The 3 direct routes

Your very first priority. These routes target the main dream. Just like how a destination can have many routes. We need to have that ready to map out. 3 ways to reach the same goal. It could be a shortest route, a traditional route, and a zig-zag route that will get you there. All these work for the same goal directly. You just need to see which fits your situation the best and know when to shift to the next if the first one isn't going your way.

Let's say you want to have your dream job in your dream company, in your dream country. There are multiple routes to get all these three together at once. Apply to your situations.

(4-6)
The 3 indirect Aid routes

Now we have another 3 steps, these are not directly related to the goal but will assist you in reaching those goals. So that's what these next three ways are, they are all about any skill or adventure that might assist in some way. Help you in having that remarkable turnaround.

All these are indirect routes that will assist you in getting on the right track. While these may not always lead to exactly where you want, it will be very close to it. Rather you may even do something new, a new idea, or a new opportunity that excites you.

You want to target the same dream job in your dream company, in your dream country. If you don't get all these three together at once you can plan to get there eventually through different routes. Maybe you can start your own company?

(7-9)
The 3 new routes

Now the next three are completely unrelated to your first priority. These are rather your second and third choice careers/lifestyles. The back-ups. It may happen that what you wanted initially isn't something you want any more, what you felt would be the best fit for you turned out to be just not working out greatly. Now this is where these back-ups come into play.

These are not always completely new things but rather related to the ones we already went through during our discussion of financial independence and having different colored baskets. You know the new ideas/hobbies we talked about before? These will be the backup.

These will be new destinations you can go to if you no longer want to work for the first anymore, you reached the first goal but realized now you want something different, or simply because the first goal was something that seemed to not be suited for you.

In the end, you want happiness. Choose that.
Choose what makes you the most happy.

A special message to all the screwed-up minds.

You can be someone who had a difficult childhood, issues with your father, mother, siblings, or friends, who have faced some trauma, dealt with things adults should have taken care of, forced to become adults in your childhood, those who still have not found there place yet in this world, who struggle to fit in, and who even struggle to genuinely smile. You know it's a fake smile you put on every day, you don't remember when you last smiled. All days just feel dull and monotonous.

I know you feel out of place especially when a person talks about his picture perfect family, the perfect career, or the perfect lifestyle (Or just open Linkedin/Instagram) and you smile but surely can't relate to it, and can't help envy. Just remember humans have a habit of sharing their success more than failure. The only time you will see a person sharing their failures is once they become successful. That way no one can judge them anymore, and no one can say anything that will hurt them anymore. It's just to protect oneself.

All of us are screwed up in some way, I don't mean it in a negative way at all.

Imagine if a typical brain has ABC all in the right order, looks great right, sure. Now when it comes to those who have screwed-up minds. It's a head of jumbled up ABCs, nothing is in the right order. But there is a big difference in how we look at it.

You can just feel bad about it or take a breath and see why it needed to be in any order in the first place? Don't we rather jumble up our alphabet to make words in the first place? Isn't messing up the order what we need? Without that, what words do you get? None. What would even be the purpose of having alphabets in the first place?

So don't let your screwed-up heads be the reason for you not to love yourself. To think you don't have what it takes, to assume you wouldn't get there. You have all the right things needed. The order isn't important. Rather, you may end up finding some new words, too.

I wrote this book to hopefully inspire some people and hopefully make you chuckle too in between. I hope I got that done successfully. I wanted all of us to not just read this book, reflect on things for a while, discuss, share (Please do), reread, and then just forget it. I want all of us to make a commitment, but remembering some of you guys' commitment issues let go with a pledge instead.

Make a pledge that starting from today when you read this, your life is to be lived as the person you envision yourself in the next 12 years. Work on your goals, make a track, write things down, learn like crazy and if plan A doesn't work, start plan B and have even more backups just in case (the 3-6-9 system). And most crucially be stubborn and be a little blazing so that when life gives you lemons, you can throw them back and make it give you the sweet fruits of your hard work.

12 years guys, I am checking on you again after 12 years. I will work toward my goals and start my journey. I want you to do the same. Let's see all we can achieve in the next 12 years and who we become in the next 12 years.

Let's see each other again then. We'll share our stories, our journeys and all we finally became. On the next blank pages write down your goals and 12 years later we will open this together again.

I'll give you head pats too, so don't disappoint me! Okay, maybe virtual head pats? It still counts! Or let's be creative! And just place this book on your head till you feel its warmth and remember someone is here for you!

Goals

12 Years target

www.ingramcontent.com/pod-product-compliance
Lightning Source LLC
LaVergne TN
LVHW091227150826
845673LV00003B/1048

* 9 7 9 8 8 9 6 9 9 5 5 0 0 *